D1053137

The LITTLE BOOK *of*
Coaching

ALSO BY KEN BLANCHARD AND DON SHULA

Everyone's a Coach

ALSO BY KEN BLANCHARD
Big Bucks!
Gung Ho!
Raving Fans
(all with Sheldon Bowles)

The One Minute Manager
(with Spencer Johnson)

Ken Blanchard
and Don Shula

The LITTLE BOOK *of*

Coaching

Motivating People to Be Winners

HarperCollins*Business*
An Imprint of HarperCollins*Publishers*

HarperCollins*Business*
An imprint of HarperCollins*Publishers*
77–85 Fulham Palace Road,
Hammersmith, London W6 8JB

www.fireandwater.com/business

Published by HarperCollins*Publishers* 2001
1 3 5 7 9 8 6 4 2

Published in the USA by HarperCollins Publishers Inc.

A catalogue record for this book
is available from the British Library

ISBN 0 00 711770 1

Printed and bound in Great Britain by
Clays Ltd, St Ives plc

TO:

*Everyone who has the opportunity
to help others accomplish their
goals through effective coaching*

ACKNOWLEDGEMENTS

Special thanks to:

CHARLIE MORGAN, for seeing the potential power of our partnership and persisting until we sat down together and started our first book, *Everyone's a Coach*, and **JIM BALLARD** for his writing support, creativity, and commitment to that book.

MIKE LIPKIN, a great motivational speaker from South Africa, for his support and love of our work and beautiful summary of the essence of each of the five secrets in the C.O.A.C.H. acronym in the launch issue 2000 of the magazine *Motivation of Champions*.

JASON ARNOLD, one of the rising stars at The Ken Blanchard Companies, for taking the first shot at putting *The Little Book of Coaching* together. This book would have never happened without his talent and initiative.

EDWIN TAN, our editor at HarperCollins, for taking over this project in midstream with enthusiasm and patience, ADRIAN ZACKHEIM, the guru of HarperBusiness, and MARGRET MCBRIDE, the Goddess of Literary Agents, for continually believing in this project and pushing for its completion.

And finally, MARGIE BLANCHARD and MARY ANNE SHULA, our partners and best friends, for always being there for us in so many ways. We love you.

Introduction

Most of you reading this book are not football coaches and never will be. But whether you're a teacher or a committee chairperson, a sales manager or a choir director, a Little League coach or a military officer, you can improve your ability to get the best performance from people.

Football and business are different, of course, but these days, the challenge for business people is not entirely different from what a coach faces on the football field. The strategy is similar—finding and using the edge that makes a difference require constant attention.

In the end, whether it's sports or business, the difference between winning and losing doesn't depend on trick plays or using new systems each week. The competition has the same information as you do. So, what are you going to use to win? *It's a matter of motivating people to prepare and work hard to play as a team.* In a word, it's coaching.

Don Shula

Leaders come and go on the American landscape. There aren't many examples of people who have sustained success in their organizations over a long period of time in this kind of pressure-cooker environment, where evaluation goes on week by week. Somehow, Don Shula was able to do it. As you read about his coaching philosophy and begin to understand how his coaching principles apply to the workplace, you will come to the conclusion that all organizations are moving closer to what Shula and top football coaches face in their jobs.

Today there are no guarantees. If your organization doesn't take care of your customers and perform well, there's somebody out there who will. The pressure is on for people to perform at their best, so there has never been a greater need for effective coaching. Regardless of whether you have an official title, there are people out there who need your help. *Everybody's a coach in some aspect of their lives, and that means you, too.*

Ken Blanchard

C.O.A.C.H. to Win

Now that you've begun to learn about what we think it takes to be successful, we want to help you put some of this philosophy into action on a day-to-day basis. Just as we did with our book *Everyone's a Coach*, we've organized the key points of *The Little Book of Coaching* into a simple acronym: C.O.A.C.H.

Each letter stands for one of the five secrets of coaching, combining what Don practiced and what Ken has taught over three decades.

*C*onviction-Driven: Never compromise your beliefs

*O*verlearning: Practice until it's perfect

*A*udible-Ready: Know when to change

*C*onsistency: Respond predictably to performance

*H*onesty-Based: Walk your talk

In this book, we use a tag team format. First, one of us shares a quote associated with a C.O.A.C.H. secret and comments about it, and then the other does the same. We want you to hear both of our voices and philosophies of coaching. So grab your whistle and clipboard and let's get in the game.

Ken Blanchard and Don Shula

Conviction-Driven

*Effective leaders
stand for something.*

What do you stand for? If we asked your colleagues, team members, or clients what your principles are, would they be able to tell us? What is the main message you broadcast to people based on your daily actions and words? Remember, *if you don't stand for something, you'll fall for anything.*

Think about your own mission and values and share them with the people around you. Think about the values of your team or your organization. Do you have core values that guide the behavior of the group? If you don't, start working on them now. Get the opinions of people around you. Have a common vision, and everyone will begin to move in the same direction.

Ken Blanchard and Don Shula

The problem with most leaders is that they don't stand for anything. And yet, leadership implies movement toward something— a sense of direction.

The realization of a dream like the Miami Dolphins' 1972 undefeated season is invariably the result of a strong set of operating beliefs and principles that are continually evident throughout the formation, training, and day-to-day practice of a team.

As a coach, I always carried with me a set of core beliefs, values, and convictions that supported my vision of perfection. These beliefs drove my entire philosophy of coaching. They set the context and boundaries from which players and coaches could operate.

You can't be a successful leader if you don't have a clear idea of what you believe, where you're headed, and what you're willing to go to the mat for. These beliefs were at the heart of everything I did with my coaches and players on the way to building a team that won consistently over many years.

Don Shula

Beliefs and convictions provide the boundaries and direction that people want and need in order to perform well.

Someone watching a football team consistently pull off brilliant plays might wonder if that kind of success is simply a matter of knowing more about the game, being more creative, or having better players or a better playbook.

Without downplaying the importance of those factors, successful coaching has more to do with the coach's own beliefs in the long run. If you're going to be a good coach, you may have to set aside the fascination with game and science and look first at what's true for you.

Beliefs are what make things happen. Beliefs come true. Inadequate beliefs are setups for inadequate performance. And it's the coach's—the leader's—beliefs that are the most important, because they become self-fulfilling.

Ken Blanchard

A river without banks
is a large puddle.

When you apply that saying to human interaction, it should remind you of your job as a coach. Like those river banks, a good coach provides the direction and concentration for performers' energies, helping channel all their efforts toward a single desired outcome.

Without that critical influence, the best achievements of the most talented performers can lack the momentum and drive that push them into becoming champions. *Over the course of my career, the one single vision of perfection that motivated all of my coaching was winning every football game.* If you don't seek perfection, you can never reach excellence.

Without exception, every coaching strategy I ever adopted was aimed at that one target. A broad target that's easy to achieve leads to the "puddle" of mediocrity. Keeping that specific focus before the team and concentrating their efforts within narrowly defined limits are the tasks of any coach.

Don Shula

Make sure everyone knows
what the target is.

Wins are a by-product of hard work—doing your best every day, every week, every year. From the moment I started coaching the Miami Dolphins in 1970, my day-to-day plan was very specific.

I wanted to make sure that my team came out of every meeting a little more intelligent than when they went in, that they came off the practice field a little better prepared mentally and physically to play the game than they were before practice. I wanted my players to make the most of every meeting, every practice, and every preseason game in order to get them ready for the regular season.

What produced winning football teams for us over the years was our willingness to create practice systems and procedures that were aligned with our vision of perfection: *We wanted to win them all.* Everything I did was to prepare people to perform to the best of their ability so they could aim for that target. And you do that one day at a time.

I believe if you want to hit a target you should aim for the bull's eye. If you aim for the bull's eye and miss, you'll still hit the target. But if you are aiming only for the target and miss, you're nowhere. Maybe it was because I regarded an unbeaten NFL season as a possibility that the feat became a reality. In 1972 the Miami Dolphins won every game, including the Super Bowl. That was the thrill of a lifetime. You may ask, "How can you do any better than that? How can you be better than perfection?" Well, you can't. But it certainly set a standard that no one could forget and one toward which I wanted my teams to always strive.

Don Shula

I experienced a perfect example of Shula's "bull's eye philosophy" when Don and I and our wives Margie and Mary Anne journeyed to Scotland to play golf a few years ago. The first course we played was Turnberry, where they have held the British Open several times.

Now, when I play golf I am a hooker—not a happy hooker, but a right-handed player who tends to hit the ball from right to left. On the first tee, I really belted a big drive, but gradually it began to hook and I ended up off the fairway in deep rough on the left.

My caddy was an older Scottish gentleman who had been caddying for years. He said, "Laddie, when you hit your driving club aim for a specific spot on the fairway. If you miss that spot, you'll probably still be on the fairway but if you just aim for the fairway, and miss that, you'll be where we are laddie, in big trouble."

Ken Blanchard

Without vision,
the people perish.

Proverbs 29:18

The reason leaders today must begin with a strong vision, and a set of positive beliefs that support it, is that without them the people they're coaching not only will lose, but will be lost. Lacking something to uplift their hearts when difficulties arise, their minds will not be equal to the challenge.

A clear vision and set of operating values are really just a picture of what things would look like if everything was running as planned and the vision was being fulfilled. World-class athletes often visualize themselves breaking a world record, pitching a perfect game, or making a 99-yard punt return before they accomplish it. They know that power comes from having a clear mental picture of their best performance potential.

It is exceedingly important for a leader of any organization to communicate his or her vision constantly to ensure that there is no doubt about the direction a team is heading. Week in and week out, the difference between success and mediocrity is often how deep an organization's leaders can get that vision to inspire people to be their best.

Ken Blanchard

Success is not forever,
and failure isn't fatal.

This was my favorite quote when I was head coach for the Miami Dolphins. It drove a great deal of my behavior during my long career.

I had a twenty-four-hour rule. I allowed myself, my coaches, and our players a maximum of twenty-four hours after a football game to celebrate a victory or bemoan a defeat. During that time, everyone was encouraged to experience the thrill of victory or the agony of defeat as deeply as possible, while learning as much as we could from that same experience. Once the twenty-four-hour deadline had passed, we put it behind us and focused our energies on preparing for the next opponent.

Don't get a big head when you win or get too down in the dumps when you lose. Keep things in perspective. Success is not forever, and failure isn't fatal.

Don Shula

How you rebound
from a setback speaks volumes
about who you are.

I got to witness firsthand Don Shula's capacity to rebound from a setback in December 1994, when the Dolphins had a disappointing 42–31 Sunday night loss to the Buffalo Bills. A win over their arch rival would have ensured the Dolphins a play-off berth and eliminated the perennial Super Bowl contenders. The Dolphins were leading 17–7 at half-time, and then the roof caved in. I was part of a group who waited in the Shula skybox for Don to appear after the game. When he did, he looked drained and exhausted. A friend tried to give him encouragement by saying, "Don't worry, Don, you'll get them next time. I know we'll make the play-offs."

Don was quick to intervene. "What I don't need right now is a pep talk." Shula needed the space to feel the loss deeply so he could then focus his, the coaches', and the team's energy on the next opponent, Kansas City.

When I saw Don on Monday night before his weekly TV show, he was a different person. I said, "Don, you really look different than you did last night." He replied, "Why not! I only have another hour to worry about Buffalo, then I can begin to concentrate on Kansas City."

That concentration paid off for the Dolphins, especially the way they blew Kansas City out of the water, 45–21, the following Monday night and secured their play-off spot.

Ken Blanchard

Your attitude makes all the difference.

Most people would say that success is not a problem. They don't realize that success can be just as devastating, if not more so, to some people as failure is. There is an abundance of stories about sports figures, entertainers, and business leaders who went quickly to the top, only to crash and burn.

As a coach or leader, your own mental attitude toward winning and losing is key. As a leader you can't afford to let yourself be overconfident through victory or consumed by failure. Doing so tends to divert attention from the business at hand or preparing for the next step.

It sounds trite, but one of the marks of real success in life is to believe that there's a reason for everything. We can't control every event, but we can control our response to it. Life is unpredictable. What makes a winner is that when something happens, that person's belief system brings forth attitudes that can take good events and make them better; likewise, it transforms bad events into opportunities to learn.

Ken Blanchard

Character is the sum total
of what you believe
and how you act.

You win with good people. It is just as important as ability. The more you as a coach know about your people, the better prepared you are to determine whether a new person will fit into your vision and create good chemistry with the rest of the team.

During the Miami Dolphins' perfect season, Nick Buoniconti was the classic overachiever. Technically, Nick wasn't big enough, fast enough, or strong enough to play linebacker, but with his great determination, enthusiasm, and love for football, he was one of the best who ever played the game. Sometimes that kind of spirit and energy can become contagious and is the type of character every coach should want to be associated with.

In today's business world, if you want to be successful, you need to have people of character who act according to the vision and values you believe in. If you don't have people who have the inner character you want, you're constantly distracted. And in today's world you can't leave character to chance.

Don Shula

One who has mastered the art of living simply pursues his vision of excellence at whatever he does, leaving others to decide whether he is working or playing.

James Michener

Work is thought of as something that you have to do, while play is something you choose to do. The distinction is more of an idea than a reality, since both require physical and mental energy. The best coaches and managers in the world are those who absolutely love what they're doing.

The enjoyment of coaching is not a perk; it's an essential ingredient of winning. People want to see that passion in a leader; it's inspiring to think that all this commitment and energy are behind your team's performance. You can't fake your love of the game; it's there or it's not. If you find you enjoy leading people to success, give it all you've got. If not, let someone else do it.

The crux of a mission statement is identifying what it is you enjoy so much that you lose track of time when you're doing it. Part of that mission must also require the desire to make a difference in other people's lives. You can achieve greater success in your responsibilities as a leader when your mission statement keeps reminding you of your passions while making important decisions regarding your career and your people.

Ken Blanchard

Overlearning

*Effective leaders help their teams
achieve practice perfection.*

Have you ever watched a real pro perform? Have you ever watched a superstar play basketball, football, soccer, or baseball? Have you ever heard a great speaker? Doesn't it look easy? Doesn't it seem as though it's effortless?

Well, it seems that way because the people whom you're watching have trained hard to get to that level. They have invested so much energy in preparing to perform that when they actually get to perform, they are ready. Remember, there is no easy walk to excellence. You and your team have to train so hard that you are almost perfect on the day of the game. The best of the best know that there is no such thing as a shortcut. All great results are built on the foundation of practice and preparation.

So get overprepared and help your people do the same.

Ken Blanchard and Don Shula

If you're going to compete today and be the best, you have to push yourself and others—hard.

When I coached my goals were the same every year. First of all, I wanted my team to qualify for the play-offs. Secondly, I wanted us to win the play-offs and get into the Super Bowl. And finally, I wanted to win the Super Bowl, which is symbolic of the world championship. If I had my way, we would have won every football game. That goal was far from everybody's mind, however, when I took over the Dolphins in 1970. The year before, their record had been 3–8–1. Our first preseason was cut short by a strike. When the team finally got to practice, I presented to the squad a plan that would make the most of every waking minute to get us ready to play football. We would have four workouts a day, following this schedule:

7:00 A.M.	PRACTICE 1: Work on special teams and kicking game
7:45 A.M.	Breakfast
9:30 A.M.	Meeting to cover morning practice points
10:00 A.M.	PRACTICE 2: Work on running game—both offense and defense
11:30 A.M.	Lunch
3:00 P.M.	PRACTICE 3: Work on passing game—both offense and defense
6:00 P.M.	Dinner
7:30 P.M.	PRACTICE 4: Work until dark on making corrections
9:30 P.M.	Meeting
10:30 P.M.	Adjourn

My players couldn't believe what I was asking them to do. There was a lot of moaning and groaning from the guys. "Four practices a day!" "This is unheard of." "What's he trying to do, kill us?" But also a few laughs. "All we're doing is dressing and undressing. What are we, ballplayers or strippers?"

When we won our first preseason game, there was less complaining. After we'd won a few more preseason games, and the press asked the players the reason for the turnaround, they all attributed it to the hard work we'd done to get ourselves ready to compete. The things they had complained the most about they later credited for the change in the football team. Incidentally, we went on to win ten games that season and were in the Super Bowl the next season.

Don Shula

Today's leading organizations share a commitment to constant improvement. They believe they're going to be better tomorrow than they were yesterday, better next week than last week, better next month than last month, and better next year than they were last year. If you're going to compete today and be the best, you have to push yourself and others—hard. Few people want to be pushed, but they need to be.

You may have had a similar experience when setting boundaries for children or pushing them to do what's required. Most kids, however, come to feel later on that what you did made an important and valuable difference in their lives.

When you make people work hard or do something they don't want to do, they don't like it. But I learned from Don Shula that if you allow sloppy practice and don't push your team to improve continually, sloppiness becomes a habit, and then it's tougher to get the team to focus on getting better when it most needs to. The best way to continue to improve is to practice hard all the time.

Ken Blanchard

It is not enough to stare up
the steps—we must step up
the stairs.

Vance Havner

Performance at the highest level should be the ultimate goal for every team. Coaching is not simply a matter of mathematics. Instead, when the whole team is on and all the pistons are firing together in synch, synergy kicks in, making the team much more than just the sum of its parts. Perfection happens only when the mechanics are automatic, and overlearning is the only way to make that happen.

Overlearning means that the players are so prepared for a game that they have the skill and confidence needed to make the big play. More than anything else, overlearning—constant practice, constant attention to getting the details right every time—produces hunger to be in the middle of the action. When players have absolutely no doubt about what they're supposed to do or how to do it, they thrive on pressure.

The way leaders, coaches, managers, or parents treat people is powerfully influenced by what they expect of people. People generally respond well to leaders who have high expectations and genuine confidence in them. Overlearning causes people to play at a higher level of expectations, raising the standards for everyone.

Don Shula

✦ ✦ ✦ ✦ ✦ ✦

Entering the hospital, the man takes an elevator to the second floor and asks for directions at the nurses' station. His face is solemn as he walks down the hallway toward the designated room. He enters and moves toward the bandaged figure on the bed. The patient sees him, smiles wanly, raises an arm from which tubes dangle.

"Thanks for coming, Coach."

"How you doing?"

"Oh, okay." The mournful look in the sunken eyes tells a different story.

There is a long pause. Finally the visitor leans in, jaw jutting close to the face of the patient.

"Listen, Mike, I need you in training camp in July—on the field, ready to go. We're going all the way this year."

✦ ✦ ✦ ✦ ✦ ✦

Later Mike Westhoff, recovered from bone cancer and still the special teams coach for the Dolphins, would say of Shula, "I thought he would have tucked me in but he didn't. He treated me the way I could be, not the way I was, and that made all the difference in the speed of my recovery."

I ask people all the time, "Given the amount of time you spend at work, would you rather spend that time being magnificent or ordinary?" What do you think they say? They shout out, "Magnificent!" And yet, are most of the people in organizations performing magnificently? Of course not. And a key reason is the self-fulfilling prophecy that starts in leaders', managers', coaches', and parents' heads, with the belief that most people are lazy, unreliable, and irresponsible. This belief plays out in how they treat people, and ultimately in how these people perform.

Is there any wonder that Don Shula was successful in getting the most out of people? His overlearning system demanded high performance from his players. His expectations of his coaches—and even of the referees—kept them constantly "performing up." He was always demanding of himself and others. There is no clearer example of this Shula characteristic than his treatment of special teams coach Mike Westhoff when Mike was stricken with cancer.

Ken Blanchard

Goal-setting is overrated!

That's what Don Shula first told me when I asked him what his goals for next season were. That shocked me because, after all, the first secret of *The One Minute Manager* was One-Minute Goal-Setting. What Don went on to help me re-learn was that setting goals is important, but most organizations overemphasize this process and don't pay enough attention to what needs to be done to achieve the goals.

More important than setting the goals is the follow-up— attention to detail, demand for practice perfection, and all the things that separate the teams that win from those that don't. All good performance starts with clear goals, but it's the day-to-day process of observing and monitoring your team's performance that makes the critical difference in the end.

It's in the implementation of your game plan that goals get accomplished. The game plan provides the mechanism for focusing your efforts toward the vision of perfection, being the best your organization can be. This is where the real coaching takes place. That's where Don Shula outstripped his competition.

Ken Blanchard

Perfection happens only when the mechanics are automatic.

If your people are worrying about what they should be doing, they have a tendency to hold back. You want them out there turning it loose. I wanted my players so familiar with their assignments that when the game started, they were operating on autopilot, the way you do when you drive a car. You're not thinking about what your hands and feet are supposed to be doing, you're just doing it.

The autopilot concept is important not only in sports but also in other areas, such as public speaking. When an orator is really prepared for a speech, he or she is able to improvise and be creative in ways that significantly enhance the presentation. Being able to function on autopilot frees you up to achieve higher levels of performance.

The goal of autopilot in the business world is to release people to do on their own what they've learned reflects the values, goals, and standards of the company—and to be creative the rest of the time. The manager who has an organization full of individuals who operate on autopilot has no need to direct them because they are able to direct and monitor themselves.

Don Shula

Practice does not make perfect.
Perfect practice makes perfect.

Once you've established a game plan based on your values, your goal each and every week as you prepare for the next game or event needs to be cutting down on practice errors. People in organizations should develop a fascination with what doesn't work. If you spend some valuable time concentrating on eliminating practice errors, you'll also eliminate a good amount of the second-guessing that goes on come performance time. Affirming and redirecting are where organizations secretly outstrip the competition. Every mistake should be noticed and corrected on the spot. There's no such thing as a small error or flaw that can be easily overlooked.

Managers often are not able to recognize the mistakes because they do not take the time to observe their people. They give directions, then clear the area. A good coach or manager is there to watch the performance and appropriately affirm or redirect when mistakes are made. You can't leave performance to chance. As a coach, if you let errors go unnoticed, you'll ensure that more of them will occur.

Don Shula

The *Miami Herald*'s Dave Barry once labeled this as a nightmare scenario:

You're in the express checkout lane, limit ten items. You have eleven items. Running the cash register is Don Shula.

Intensity is the theme of many Shula stories. I love the one about what happened in the Miami Dolphins locker room a number of years ago after a game against the New York jets. The Dolphins had won, but Shula was not pleased with their play. He had a few choice words he wanted to share with the team. (Mel Philipps, who coaches the defensive backs, told me, "Don is sometimes tougher on the team when they win than when they lose. He knows that the team is stronger when we've won and that when we lose, they're already feeling bad enough.") As he entered the locker room to speak to the players, Shula saw someone he didn't recognize. "Who the hell is that?" he shouted. Someone answered, "He's a writer." "Get him out of here!" Shula commanded. With that, James Michener, who was working on his book *Sports in America,* left the Dolphins locker room. At that moment Don Shula could not have cared less.

In all the time I spent with Don Shula working on this book he never permitted me in the locker room. That was where he talked privately with his players and coaches.

Ken Blanchard

People say I was intense as a coach. I didn't know how to behave differently. I believed in what I did. I had the courage of my conviction. I demanded discipline. I don't keep anything inside me. What you see is what you get. Sometimes I wasn't very proud of what came out, but at least it didn't stay inside. I guess I wasn't afraid to let fly because I wanted to use that energy to build emotional response. I didn't ever want it said after a game that our opponent's emotions ran higher than ours or that they wanted the game more than we did.

On October 2, 1994, I had the opportunity to play against my son, David, who was coaching the Cincinnati Bengals at the time. This was the first matchup in any sport between father and son coaches. It was a special day and one I'll always remember. I was also happy when it was over and we had won. My wife, Mary Anne, was the only member of my family who was rooting for the Dolphins. My kids felt that David needed the victory more than I did. In my heart I might have agreed with them, but my responsibility was to the Dolphins. I couldn't let family feelings enter into the game. I wanted to see David win, and win a lot. I just didn't want to see him win that Sunday.

Don Shula

Intensity is measured by a person's level of will and passion to do whatever it takes to get the job done successfully. The intensity to strive for continual improvement matters as never before in today's business world. If you're not willing to push your people to constantly improve, you can be sure your competitors will.

Any level of successful leadership demands that same type of consistent intensity that led Don Shula to become the NFL's winningest coach. His first win in 1970 was no different from his 325th in 1995; however, it was the culmination of his consistent passion to strive for continuous improvement that put up the Hall of Fame numbers.

Today's leading organizations share a common commitment to constant improvement. They believe they're going to be better tomorrow than they were yesterday, better next week than last week, better next month than last month, and better next year than last year.

Ken Blanchard

Audible-Ready

*Effective leaders, and the people and teams
they coach, are ready to change when the
situation demands it.*

In today's world, nothing stays the same. The "cheese" is always moving. Being audible-ready means being ready to switch strategies and game plans whenever it's necessary. That means you and your team members need the vital quality of flexibility—the ability to bond and flow with change.

Many people are struggling right now because they haven't learned the power of flexibility. They are still living in the past. They are scared to move forward. You know why? Because they do not have the confidence to do so. They are afraid of failure. They are fearful of looking stupid. They doubt themselves. They are stuck in a rut.

As a coach, you need to help those around you to become flexible. From today, ensure that you're flexible enough to adapt to new realities and help others to do the same.

Ken Blanchard and Don Shula

If your enemy is superior, evade him. If angry, irritate him. If equally matched, fight. If not, retreat and reevaluate.

Sun Sioux proverb

An audible is a verbal command that tells your players to substitute new assignments for the ones they were prepared to perform. Today's leaders can't afford to sit around afterward learning what they should have done; they need to be ready to do whatever it takes to win the game, serve their clients, or protect their families.

Part of readiness is the ability to shift your game plan at will, as a battlefield commander who has the guts to make the right moves in the heat of combat. Prepare well with a plan—then expect the unexpected and be ready to change that plan. As a leader you must preserve the right to change plans—even to change them at the last moment—as circumstances may dictate.

Audibles are not last-minute orders dreamed up out of nowhere. They're strategies your team knows about and has practiced thoroughly before the call is made. In the fast-paced technological world of today, organizations must be "audible ready"—not only to change a play or two but to change the entire game plan if necessary.

Don Shula

Adaptation is not allowing yourself
to give in to circumstances;
it's allowing those circumstances to
give you success.

Audibles aren't surprises—just new ways of doing what you already know how to do. Businesspeople need to learn to call audibles, because in today's world, nothing stays the same very long.

Many organizations today have an organizational chart with everyone in a comfortable box. It might look nice on the wall, but it locks everyone into a fixed game plan and often into fixed rules. It doesn't give the organization the power to respond quickly to new demands that occur in business. It's the companies that are constantly adapting that are making striking advances today.

More and more companies are scrambling to get into the position that Shula's football teams did under his command: the ability to substitute plays and formations at will in order to get the job done in a changing environment. The ability of nimble service corporations to transfer their energies quickly in order to solve a customer's problem or meet a market's sudden need is the very characteristic Shula calls "audible ready."

Ken Blanchard

For waging war, you need guidance, and for victory—many advisers.

Proverbs 24:6

There is no point in sticking with a game plan that's not working. The sun does not rise and fall based on one person's judgment. Effective coaches are continually out there scanning for data and advice that will make their decisions more intelligent.

I made my offensive and defensive coordinators and assistant coaches responsible for their own areas and for communicating with their players. It was their job to relay any pertinent information that surfaced during the practice week or during the game.

Good coaches listen to their staff, and once they've heard all of the important information, they're prepared to make the best decisions under any circumstance. With many counselors, audibles aren't surprises—just new ways of doing what you already know how to do.

Don Shula

Be prepared with a plan and then expect the unexpected and be ready to change your plan.

Of all the bureaucratic departments I've had to deal with over the years, the Department of Motor Vehicles (DMV) has to have been the most dreary and demeaning. I used to think the DMV hired only employees who hated people; they seemed to take delight in telling customers they were in the wrong line or had filled out a form incorrectly. I always tried to avoid direct interaction with the DMV, but several years ago, three weeks before I was due to go to Europe, I lost my driver's license. Needing to get the renewal procedure going fast so that my new license could serve as a backup to my passport, I asked Dana Kyle, my executive assistant (who ran my life at the time), to schedule a three-hour block of time at the DMV. I figured that was about the amount of time they needed to beat me up properly.

I headed to the DMV, fully expecting the same old treatment, but to my surprise, I found that a transformation had occurred. As I entered, a woman employee greeted me: "Welcome to the Department of Motor Vehicles. Do you speak English or Spanish?" Taken aback, I mumbled, "English." She ushered me to a counter, where I was met by a smiling young man who asked how he could help me. When the procedure was over I had my new license, the total time—including having my picture taken—had been nine minutes!

"What are you all smoking here?" I asked the woman taking my photo. "This isn't the DMV I used to know and love!"

"Have you met our new boss?" she asked, smiling and pointing to a desk situated smack in the middle of the service area. I walked over to say hello to a pleasant middle-aged man who told me his role was to "reorganize the department on a moment to moment basis, depending on citizen need." As we talked, I saw that he was a man who obviously enjoyed his work, took pride in his organization, and cherished a vision of building a customer service organization. His commitment to doing whatever it takes to get the job done well—the job of serving citizens—was obvious. For instance, he didn't schedule any employee's lunch break between 11:30 A.M. and 2:00 P.M. because that's when most people tend to visit the DMV office. He'd also cross-trained the staff, including the secretaries in the back offices, so that anyone could take photos or serve at the front desk. If the number of customers suddenly increased, he could swiftly reorganize the office to meet the demand. This guy knows what it means to be audible-ready. Do you?

Ken Blanchard

Sometimes something will happen beyond your control, like an injury to a key player, and that requires you to change not just an occasional play but your whole game plan.

In 1965 when I was coaching the Baltimore Colts, our all-star quarterback, Johnny Unitas, was out with injuries, and so was our backup quarterback, Gary Cuozzo. Both were great passers, but I had no other quarterbacks on the team, so I used Tom Matte, a halfback, as quarterback in the play-offs. Tom had had some quarterback experience at Ohio State, but back then, under Woody Hayes's offensive philosophy ("three yards and a cloud of dust"), the quarterback was mainly a blocking back. I changed the game plan to take advantage of Matte's running strength, and it worked. Tom didn't know the plays from quarterback, so we ended up writing them on his wristband.

We won a crucial game against the L.A. Rams, earning ourselves a play-off shot at the Western Division crown, against Green Bay. One of Matte's famous wristbands resides today in the Football Hall of Fame in Canton, Ohio. I've got the other one in my office. It reminds me that you have to "move with the cheese."

Don Shula

◆

Consistency

Effective leaders are predictable in their response to performance.

* * * * * *

The Miami blitz is on. A defensive tackle breaks through the offensive line and nails the quarterback for an eight-yard loss. The opponent will have to kick on fourth down. Shula is the first one to greet the tackle as he comes off the field. "Nice job!"

It's third and three. The hand-off is to the running back. He slices through an opening in the line, sidesteps a linebacker and cuts for the sidelines. It's a footrace, and he wins. Miami touchdown! Wait, there's a flag down on the forty. Oh no! Holding called on Miami. Forget the touchdown. The look on Coach Shula's face suggests you would not want to be the offender.

* * * * * *

With great coaches, the treatment of individuals is predictable. Their focus is always on getting people to be their best. Their consistency is legendary. If performance is going well, they're ready to praise, but if the team or an individual isn't living up to these coaches' expectations, they are ready to redirect or reprimand. They behave the same way again and again in similar circumstances. It's not the mood they're in but people's performance that dictates their response.

Ken Blanchard and Don Shula

Consistency is not behaving the same way all the time; it is behaving the same way in similar circumstances.

Most people have the wrong idea about consistency. They think it means behaving the same way all the time. If you praise people and are nice to them when they're performing well and also when they are behaving poorly, that's inconsistent. Consistency is behaving the same way in similar circumstances.

Your players need to be able to count on your consistency. What we're talking about here is a specific kind of consistency—a consistency in responding to people's performance. When you respond to your players in the same way under similar circumstances, you give them the valuable gift of predictability.

With this type of consistency your team will quickly learn what your standards are and perform accordingly. You need to be down on the field every day, smelling out whatever isn't working. Even the slightest deviation from perfection needs to be noticed and corrected on the spot. A winning coach can't afford to let the little things go unnoticed because that often spells the difference between success and failure.

Don Shula

Behavior is controlled by the consequence or response it receives.

There are four consequences or responses people can receive after they perform or do something. The most common response people get for their performance is no response. They do something and no one says anything. The next most common response is negative—they get zapped. As a result, many managers are seen as "seagull managers." They are not around until something goes wrong and then they fly in, make a lot of noise, dump on people, and then fly out. Not a very helpful way to be managed.

The last two responses—redirection and positive—are the least used and yet most effective. When someone does something wrong, redirection focuses his or her energy back on what the original goal was. A positive consequence is welcome when a person does something right or makes progress. When something positive follows people's good performance, they will want to repeat that good performance in the future.

Avoid being a "leave alone and zap" manager and use redirect and praising more.

Ken Blanchard

You can't catch your people doing something right if you're not there to see them doing something right.

A no-response consequence occurs when nothing is said or done following the action. Good actions that receive no recognition at all are apt to be discarded eventually; bad actions will continue unchanged. The only exception is when people are self-actualizing, that is, when they love what they're doing and will continue to do it well regardless of whether they receive any recognition.

In the typical organization, the most frequent response people get to their performance is no response. Why? Because most managers are not around to see their people doing something right.

When I missed practice to have my Achilles tendon repaired in 1994, the press made a big deal over the fact that it was the first practice I had missed in my twenty-five years with the Dolphins. But I didn't understand why people made such a fuss. To me it was inconceivable to be absent when the team was practicing. Good coaching means being present, on the spot, constantly giving appropriate feedback on your players' performance. I just don't think you can coach from the press box.

Don Shula

One thing I never wanted to be
accused of was not noticing.

Don Shula

The coaches are allowed to walk up and down the sidelines between the 35 yard lines only, but Shula sometimes forgot. Occasionally I found him all the way down to the 5 yard line. He wanted to be lined up nose-to-nose right on the line of scrimmage, so he could see what was happening. He was amazing. He would see simultaneously what the offense and the defense were doing. He could read the defense, and he knew where the opposing quarterback ought to be throwing; if the quarterback threw to the wrong spot, he knew that. He had incredible knowledge of the game. He could see all twenty-nine people at the same time—twenty-two players and seven officials. He knew what they were all supposed to be doing and when they were supposed to be doing it. It was unbelievable.

Jim Tunney,
NFL official for over thirty years and co-author of
Chicken Soup for the Sports Fan's Soul

Studies show that among teenagers, there are significantly less incidents of drinking, drug use, indiscriminate sex, and fatal traffic accidents occurring before 12:00 midnight than after that hour. Suppose that the parents of a sixteen-year-old learn about this and say, "We'd better get our son home earlier." They announce to him, in no uncertain terms, that they want him home by midnight. The next time he's out with his friends and sees it is 11:30 P.M., he says, "My parents want me in by twelve, I've got to leave." His peers start shaming him: "What are you, man, a momma's boy? Are they going to tuck you in?" He's getting a negative response from his all-important peer group. He's a good kid, though, so he bears the negative response and says, "No, I've gotta go." But when he walks in the door on time at home, where are his parents? They're either gone or asleep. He's lucky if he gets a lick from the dog. This is a typical no-response.

Now let's see how the "leave-alone" results in a "zap!" First, let's look at the score in terms of who has noticed what: so far, the teenager has one negative response (from his peers) and one no-response (from his parents). Which will have the greater effect? Negative noticing will win. It's no contest. Most people will be impacted more by a negative response than by a no-response. This is why it's so important to be there to praise good behavior. In some companies we give managers a set of buttons that read, "I was caught doing something right" and tell them to give a button to an employee when they notice good performance. The recipients appreciate this.

If this is a typical no-response case, what happens when the boy goes out the next night? At 11:30 when he makes his announcement that he needs to be home by midnight, his friends start in on him again. This time he thinks to himself, "Am I crazy? I got home last night on time and nobody noticed. Why should I take this grief from my buddies?" Tonight he arrives home at 1:00 A.M. Where are his parents this time? They're at the door yelling at him, "We told you to be home by twelve! We're sick and tired of your lousy attitude." Seagull management in action. This puts the kid in a lose–lose situation: if he does what his parents want, he gets beat up by his friends; if he does what his friends want, he gets grief from his folks.

The only way to turn this situation around is for his parents—the managers in this case—to start to accentuate the positive and catch him doing something right. If you want your children to be home by a certain hour, do whatever it takes to be there to reward their good behavior. If you're asleep, set an alarm. If you're out with friends, announce to them by 11:30, "We told our son to be home by midnight, and we want to be there when he comes home." When the kid walks in, make a big fuss over him, hugging and kissing him and making a big show of celebration. Sound corny? Guess what—it works.

Ken Blanchard

If you're going to take the time to do what's urgent, be sure to take time to recognize what's important.

A positive consequence is when something good (from the receiver's perspective) occurs—for example, a praising, a recognition, a raise, or a bigger opportunity to perform. If a reward or positive consequence is given, the person is apt to repeat the action. People tend to move toward pleasure. Positive consequences motivate future behavior.

Recognizing good performance is an important part of coaching. Spreading out praise so that every contributor receives attention, especially those unsung heroes in some of the less visible positions, is vital to the unity of any team. Though recognition may go against your notion that coaches are effective when they're toughest and most demanding, recognizing good performance is a strategic part of a coach's game plan.

Perhaps today's leaders are too focused on doing what's urgent to take time for what's important. Once leaders, coaches, managers, and parents see that praise and recognition are directly linked to performance, they'll see them as integral parts of their job—which is, after all, getting the best out of people.

Ken Blanchard

There is no such thing as
a minor mistake.

Mistakes cannot be tolerated. If the team or individual does something wrong, the coach needs to blow the whistle, tell them what they did wrong, and make them do it again. Somehow, as a coach, you continually have to redirect your team back to the standards for good performance.

When redirection occurs, performance is stopped, and people's efforts are rechanneled to do correctly what they were doing incorrectly. If people are redirected to do something correctly, they are apt to continue doing it correctly. Redirection can be a powerful way to get people to refocus their behavior.

Redirecting is the way to correct a mistake when an individual or team has not yet learned to do what you want you want them to do. If people make a mistake while they are learning and you yell at them or punish them, you'll only increase their anxiety and motivate them to avoid the punisher—you.

Don Shula

Faithful are the wounds
of a friend.

Hebrew proverb

A negative consequence occurs when something bad (from the receiver's perspective) takes place—for example, a reprimand, a punishment, a demotion, or a removal from an activity. People tend to move away from pain. If an action produces undesirable consequences, the person is apt to avoid it.

A reprimand is an example of a negative consequence. You're telling people what they did wrong as soon as possible. A good reprimand is specific; it includes your feelings and ends by affirming the person. A coach should use a reprimand only when an individual or team has already proven that they can do what you want done, but are now falling short.

From time to time, some of the people you coach are going to test your limits. You have to pass these tests. You can't tolerate flagrant misbehavior or infractions of your rules. If you do, it sends the wrong message to the other players. But as a coach, you must be wise in your confrontations and flexible in the way you treat people at such times. When you get upset with a player or team, it is always focused on performance—not the person.

Ken Blanchard

After you deliver a reprimand, it's important for people to understand that you still value them as human beings.

When my son, Scott, was a senior in high school, he used to cause problems by parking his truck in the driveway. Nobody could get in or out because his truck was big enough to go to war. I told him to park it out in the street. One day I came home to find he'd not only blocked the driveway with his truck but had gone away and taken his keys with him. I was furious. Three hours later he showed up and I was waiting for him. I stormed out of the house and I let him have it. I didn't leave him in doubt about what he'd done wrong and how I felt about it. As I was walking back to the house, Scott raced after me. He followed me into the kitchen. "Dad," he said, "you forgot the last part of this reprimand—you know, the part about 'You're a good kid, I love you and this is so unlike you.'" I cracked up laughing. We hugged. Scott never left his truck in the driveway again. And I became better at reaffirming at the end of a reprimand.

Ken Blanchard

Honesty-Based

*Effective leaders have high integrity
and are clear and straightforward
in their interactions with others.*

Finally, and maybe most importantly, champion coaches operate out of unquestionable integrity. They call it the way they see it. They do not have hidden agendas. They do not say one thing but mean another. They do not manipulate people. They are genuine and sincere.

We promise you that you can only be at your best when you are being entirely authentic. That means you're not trying to be anybody else. You are being true to your own character. You are being honest not just with other people, but with yourself as well. Remember, if you remain true to yourself, you cannot be false to anybody else.

If you are honesty-based, you will not waste energy trying to be what you're not, or try to cover your tracks because you keep telling people different stories. In fact, only by being honesty-based can you sustain high performance. People who are not honesty-based lose the game of life, because they lose the trust of the people around them. And the moment you lose other people's trust, you lose everything.

Ken Blanchard and Don Shula

Victory if possible,
integrity at all costs.

The struggle to succeed and the hard-fought nature of a win are characteristics of the American way of life. But breaking the rules is not a part of victory. Doing something unethical or dishonest erodes a leader's image as well as self-esteem.

During Don Shula's twenty-five-year tenure as coach of the Miami Dolphins, his team was the least-penalized team in the NFL. Playing by the rules will give your team the upper hand when lodged in tight situations and moments of chaos. When everything seems lost, knowledge of the rules—and the determination to figure out a way to win the game without breaking those rules—ensures long-term success.

In a competitive environment, where it seems anything goes, ethical considerations are often the first to be abandoned. The reason this doesn't work is that the number one characteristic people are looking for in a leader is integrity. More than anything else they want to be told the truth. They want it the Shula way—straight.

Ken Blanchard

Yes, Shula is just a pro football coach, albeit the best known by virtue of those 325 victories. But the fact is, in a place that lurches from day-to-day just waiting for the next scandal, Shula's single-minded plod after George Halas has rewarded him with a status that few public figures in south Florida can claim. He is clean.

S. L. Price, Miami Herald, *special Shula edition, November 15, 1993*

Don Shula not only values honesty in himself, but also likes and respects it in others. In the last game of my first season as an NFL official, I made the worst call I'd ever made—against Shula's Baltimore Colts. They were playing the Redskins in Baltimore, and the score was tied 17–17, when in the waning minutes, Washington threw a pass into the end zone, and Rick Volk of the Colts intercepted it. On his third step, he hit a white line that I thought was the sideline. The line that Volk hit was actually a foot inside the end zone. Not knowing this at the time, I signaled a touchback as Volk raced down the field on a touchdown run of 106 yards, a run that would have broken a record that had stood since 1920. I compounded my mistake by chasing Volk down the field to get the ball. Shula and the whole Baltimore team were furious with me. A few plays later, after I'd realized my mistake, I passed by the Baltimore bench and Shula hollered, "Hey, rookie, what the hell are you doing out there?" I stopped and said, "Coach, I blew it, and I feel terrible about it."

After the game, which Baltimore lost, the reporters gathered around Shula and immediately wanted to know what he thought about my call. Shula said, "Holst came by the bench and told me that he blew it and that he felt badly. He's an honest man. Next question."

Art Holst, former NFL official

To be successful, all you have to do is work half-days; you can work the first twelve hours or the second twelve.

Never ask your people to do more than you are willing to do. As a coach, your own preparation for everything you do has to be exemplary. If you are dedicated to success and will do whatever it takes to achieve it, the rest of your team will be, too.

A lot of leaders want to tell people what to do, but they don't provide the example. "Do as I say, not as I do," doesn't cut it when leading people to a destination of success. As a coach your high standards of performance, attention to detail, and— above all—how hard you work set the stage for how your players perform.

One of the critical leadership issues in our country today is lack of respect and credibility. With the rapid changes continuing in organizations today, the typical employee sees little pain occurring at the top. Usually we're so busy with our tasks we forget that, above all else, what our people want most of all from us is *us*—our values, our attitudes, our perceptions. In the long run, it's not our skills or our know-how or our experience that makes the biggest impact—*we* are the main message!

Ken Blanchard

It takes a big person to admit a mistake and then go out of his or her way to right the wrong.

Journalist Peggy Stanton included Don Shula among nine men she profiled in her book *The Daniel Dilemma: The Moral Man in the Public Arena*. One of the reasons Stanton chose Shula as an example of a moral man is illustrated by her documented comments about his reaction to an incident when he was off base:

> Don Shula lost his temper on national television during a heated game with the Los Angeles Rams. Unhappy with the referee's call, Shula voiced his displeasure in language that did not make him proud, especially when an open microphone was carrying his whack at the Second Commandment ("Do not take the Lord's name in vain") into millions of American homes. He was flooded with letters from people all over the country telling him how he'd let them down. Everyone who included a return address received an apology from Shula expressing his regret without excuse. "Thank you for taking time to write," ran a typical response. "Please accept my apologies for the remarks. I value your respect and will do my best to earn it again."

Most football fans were familiar with Shula's jutting jaw and determined scowl as he strode up and down the sidelines, but probably few knew the soft, gentle, and vulnerable side of Don Shula. It's that side of the man that kept his ego out of the way.

Ken Blanchard

A sense of humor is simply
a sense of who you are.

There are few things better than a good laugh. A sense of humor helps you keep things in perspective. Humor also permits you to accept criticism without getting consumed by it. Criticism never becomes a life-and-death situation.

A lot of people in organizations today take themselves too seriously. A fun smile or a really good laugh is hard to find within most organizational walls. It's hard to be honest and forthright with folks whose egos and pride are always up for grabs. What we need to learn is how to laugh at ourselves first.

Without a sense of humor, we seem to stifle the child in others and ourselves. When all the emphasis in business is on whether we're doing things right or wrong, we never get to experience the delight of exclaiming, "Isn't that interesting!"

Ken Blanchard

Everyone talks about my jutting jaw and the fact that I once said, "I don't get ulcers, I give them." But there are few things I like better than a good laugh. One of my greatest joys in coaching was working with players who had a good sense of humor.

Hall of Famer Larry Csonka was this kind of guy. I have known few people who were as competitive and who showed as much leadership on the field as Csonka. While Csonka loved to play in the games, he was not always as excited about practice. Our staff sometimes had to motivate him to practice. In the press, Csonka and his buddy Jim Kiick were known as Butch Cassidy and the Sundance Kid. One time I got on them during the perfect season. I was riding them both pretty hard. I went to take a shower after practice, and when I opened the door, I found a live alligator staring me in the face! I jumped back and ran out of the shower room—straight to Csonka's locker.

"What are you guys doing?" I yelled.

Csonka smiled and said, "Don't yell at us, Coach. You should thank Jim and me, instead. The rest of the team wanted the alligator's mouth left open, but we were the only ones that voted to have the alligator's mouth taped."

This really broke me up. We all had a good laugh.

Don Shula

I was always a happy kid. Laughter was part of my growing up. I even learned that humor could also help you deal with stressful situations as well as play an important part in leadership development.

When I was growing up in New Rochelle, New York, the elementary school I was attending entered a citywide elementary basketball tournament and got into the finals. The other school had a big kid on their team by the name of Earl Forte. All of his teammates called him "Meatball."

I was always a pretty good shooter, and that day I had one of those games that you dream about—almost everything I threw up went in. We won, and after the game, I went to change my clothes. As I went by the locker where Earl was sitting, I said, "Nice game, Meatball!" He whipped around, grabbed me by the shirt and threw me against the locker. "Only my friends call me Meatball!" he shouted.

I don't know where I got the composure as a young kid, but I laughed and said, "Oh, then why don't we become friends?" He cracked up and put me down and said, "You're okay." After graduation from elementary school, we went to the same junior high school. When I ran for seventh-grade class president, Earl became one of my campaign managers. He and I remained good friends throughout our schooling together.

Ken Blanchard

Popularity is temporary.
Respect is timeless.

I remember an English teacher named Miss Symmes. All the other English teachers I had had would pat me on the back and give me a B because they liked me and wanted me to like them. Not Miss Symmes. The first essay I wrote for her she returned with an F and told me I was better than that. Since I was already a student leader, I thought I could get by with my gift for gab, but she insisted that I needed to learn to write, too. And she wouldn't back off. She pushed and pushed me until, on the last paper I turned in to her, she was proud to give me an A. I was proud, too. I'll never forget her. I bet you have a "Miss Symmes" in your life.

The bigger issue, though, is: Are you willing to be a "Miss Symmes" to someone else? Are you willing to push your players beyond their comfort zone so that they can experience excellence? Being a great coach means sacrificing popularity and being liked for doing the right thing, so that you are respected. In the long run, you'll be remembered as the best coach they ever had.

Ken Blanchard

Comments about postgame activities after the Dolphins' record-breaking game with Philadelphia on November 14, 1993:

The greatest tribute to Don Shula involved the one tribute his players would not offer Sunday. Respect for the NFL's winningest coach was leaving the Gatorade cooler on the ground. Members of the Dolphins were going to dump the liquid on their leader during the final moments of Shula's 325th career victory, a 19–14 victory over the Philadelphia Eagles. But at the last second, they changed their minds. He had just led them to a second-half comeback with their third-string quarterback. He had just convinced them, once again, to embrace the improbable. They didn't want him looking like a drowned rat. They wanted him looking like a king.

"A classy man," guard Keith Sims said. "We looked at the Gatorade and said 'You know, we need to do a classy thing.'" And so he was lifted by three linemen and carried across the Veterans Stadium field, his left arm thrust to the sky, his eyes moist, surrounded by dozens of his players straining to touch him. In passing George Halas for the most career coaching victories in NFL history, Shula traveled in style.

Bill Plasche, Los Angeles Times

The relationship I wanted to establish with my football team is one of mutual respect. I always wanted my players to respect me for giving them everything that I had to prepare them to play to the best of their ability. My respect for them came from knowing that they were willing to give me all that they had to prepare themselves to be ready to play.

The only way you can get respect is to earn it. Not by talking— but by having people see you doing things, time after time, that make sense to them. Your people have to recognize that your actions are motivated not by your ego but by your desire to have them be their best.

The same things that make up the character of a successful coach are the same things that will make you a successful parent, spouse, or manager. The moment you accept leadership responsibility, whether it's in business, education, government, or the family, the spotlight is turned your way and tough decisions are your call. As long as you have credibility, you have good leadership, and that's something people can hang their hat on—something they can immediately believe and accept.

Don Shula

I don't know any other way
to lead but by example.

Don Shula

During the 1994–95 season Don Shula ruptured his Achilles tendon. The day he had the operation was the first regular-season practice Shula had missed in his twenty-five years with the Dolphins. He fought having the operation. "I can't ask my players to play hurt if I wimp out when I'm hurting a little bit." Finally the doctors gave him no choice. Mary Anne Shula reported:

> After the operation, Don was taken to recovery and then to his hospital room, where he was scheduled to stay overnight. By 2:30 in the afternoon, he'd had enough of the hospital. He asked me for his crutches and we were on our way home shortly afterward. By 5:30 the next morning, he was up and wanting to attend Mass and then go to practice. By 10:00 A.M. he was on the practice field in a golf cart. And that was the way he coached on Monday night against the Kansas City Chiefs.

After the Chiefs had scored on long drives the first two times they had the ball, the TV cameras zoomed in on Shula directing his driver to where the defensive team sat after they came off the field. One of the commentators watching this laughed and said, "I think some of those defensive players are lucky that Shula can't get out of that golf cart. . . . If things don't get better, he might drive that cart right onto the field." After Don's outburst, the defense rose to the occasion and helped the Dolphins win this important game and play-off spot.

Ken Blanchard

Authenticity bridges the gap
between what we say and
what we do.

Effective coaches confront their people, praise them sincerely, redirect or reprimand them without apology, and, above all, are honest with them. Dealing with others in a leadership capacity will test your character, especially if your roles are highly visible. You should expect the pressures and be ready for them by becoming transparent about what you believe, what's good enough for you, and how you need to treat people in order to get the job done.

A huge amount of energy is lost in organizations by people complaining and commiserating over the lack of congruence in company leaders. There are gaps in many organizations due to the difference between what managers say they stand for and how they actually treat people.

Gaps are a problem not only in our organizations, but also in our personal lives. We say our family is important, yet the average couple in America is reported to talk to each other only seven minutes a day, while the average household has the TV on five to six hours a day. Since we all are a coach in one form or another, we all must find ways of bridging the gaps between what we say and what we do.

Ken Blanchard

People with humility don't think less of themselves . . . they just think about themselves less.

Great coaches are not consumed by their own importance. When they win, they're happy—particularly if the team performed well. When they lose, they're not happy—but they are able to put that behind them.

Fear and the need to be right dominate people who are ego-driven. They're afraid to fail because they think their worth as human beings depends on how others see them. They have to keep winning to prove they're okay. To ego-driven people, only the number of wins, sales, conquests, or acquisitions they achieve measures success. Great coaches want to win, but they don't fall apart when they lose.

One of the most destructive traits a leader can have today is arrogance—acting like you've got it together all the time. On the other hand, one of the most endearing qualities a leader can have is to be in touch with his or her vulnerability. It's that side of a leader that keeps the vision from crumbling under the pressure of circumstance.

Ken Blanchard

Belief in something bigger
than you is important.

People close to me will tell you I was not a real pleasant person after losing a football game, but I would have been a lot worse if I didn't realize that something far bigger than football exists. I tried to attend Mass every morning. There's something good about kneeling down, asking for help, and listening for answers.

If your highest authority is your boss or your organization, your last victory, or, worse, yourself, you won't be a very effective coach. With a big-picture perspective, adversity, circumstance, or even your own ego will not consume you. As a result you don't have to panic, give up, start to cheat, lose control, or begin to take uncalled-for risks to get the results you want right now.

Genuine faith is eminently practical, and that vast resource for inner knowing stands ready to assist today's leader who will exercise it. Faith in something bigger than you isn't a passive emotion; it's an active belief that requires you to step onto the field and walk your talk.

Don Shula

It's a wonder to me that practical business people avoid looking in the direction of inner or spiritual guidance for solving their problems. Somehow, organized religion has not connected the idea of God with the nitty-gritty problems people face every day. That is why I co-founded The Center for Faith Walk Leadership to help people of faith walk their faith in the marketplace. If faith in God does not help people solve baffling personnel problems that come up in their organizations, or if it serves no purpose in working through the painful issues of downsizing or cutting costs or reengineering, then what good is it? I believe that genuine faith is eminently practical, and that a vast resource for inner knowing stands ready to assist today's leaders who try it.

Good religion is like good football: it isn't talk, it's action. People aren't interested in your religious badge or your theory. They are looking for leaders whose faith works for them on a day-to-day basis.

Ken Blanchard

✦ ✦ ✦ ✦ ✦ ✦

It's early on a weekday; most people in Miami haven't had breakfast yet. The sanctuary is cool, dark, quiet. The first rays of the sun are coming through the stained-glass window, painting the stone floors with shards of color. The silence is broken only by an occasional rustle of movement or a quiet cough from the handful of parishioners who file past the altar, receiving communion. As the last of the supplicants turns away, the priest glances toward a rear pew, where a lone figure is bent in prayer. He smiles and thinks, "The Dolphins must be back in town."

✦ ✦ ✦ ✦ ✦ ✦

My mother and father were both strong-willed, intensely moral people. My mother was raised a Roman Catholic, and my father converted when he married her. A great many of the ideas and thoughts I have, as far as my relationship with God is concerned, stem from those early years and the lessons I learned around the house about honoring God and doing things the right way. For example, we never missed Mass. From second grade on, I went to a Catholic school, including college, and when I coached I tried to attend Mass every day. When we were at home, I attended a small service every morning at 6:30 A.M., conducted by Father Gelser at St. Thomas University. I had known Father Gelser ever since I arrived in Miami in 1970. Attending Mass and looking to God for guidance weren't just habits for me. They mattered deeply to me when I was out in the world of shrill whistles and clashing bodies. And when game day came, they were ways for me to keep my perspective.

Don Shula

One Final Word

The real difference in coaching is about believing in someone and then taking action to help that person be his or her very best.

"Who believed in you?" asked a management seminar leader. One participant shared his story. "When I was a teenager I took care of mowing the neighbors' lawn. When they got ready to go on a three-week vacation, they told me they were leaving me in charge of the whole place. When they gave me the house key, I felt something I'd never felt before. They believed in me, and that made me want to do the best job I could. And I did."

Who believed in you? Don had Paul Brown as his football mentor and coach. Ken Blanchard had his Miss Symmes, who saw his potential as a writer. Perhaps someone did or said something that gave you a positive shock of recognition about yourself. That person's vision of what you were capable of ignited something inside you. You said to yourself, "Well, if they think I can do it, maybe I can." You were challenged to reach down into yourself and call forth the effort that matched their vision of your potential. Lo and behold, you rose to it!

The question is: How do you create that spark of self-recognition in others? In your life you'll have coaching opportunities that are expected. They appear as a natural function of your designated role as a manager, a parent, a Little League coach, or a Girl Scout leader. The secrets in this book will help you rise to these challenges.

When Heather Whitestone won the 1994 Miss America contest, attention focused on her background. How did a girl who had been deaf since birth surpass all the other beautiful and talented contestants to earn this coveted award? Heather's secret was the belief and faith shown in her by her mother, Daphne Gray, who steadfastly refused to see her daughter's deafness as a handicap.

Daphne's belief that Heather could be anything she wanted to be was transferred to the girl, who then went on to become a peak performer. This modern-day success story echoes another well-known one: Helen Keller's teacher took someone who by society's standards at the time should have been a throw-away person, and planted and nurtured the seed of belief that anything was possible. Helen then became a woman of wisdom and an example to people everywhere.

So your roles will furnish you with naturally occurring opportunities to coach others. But don't stop there. Other chances to recognize people's potential will present themselves every day, everywhere you go—provided you keep your eyes open. When Norman Vincent Peale celebrated his 90th birthday at the Waldorf Astoria, people rose one by one to tell how important Norman had been in their lives. When the guest of honor stood up to speak, he shared an anecdote that typifies his whole life as a spiritual coach to millions. Norman said:

> On a recent plane trip I noticed that the businessman sitting next to me was looking worried. I decided to engage him in conversation.

"How are you doing?" I asked.

"Oh, not so good," was the reply.

"What's wrong?"

"I just got promoted."

'What's so bad about that?"

"I'm just not sure I've got what it takes to do the job."

"Yes you do."

"Why, how do you know?"

"You do—if you *think* you do!"

Then I told him to start each day chanting, *"Think* big! *Act* big! *Be* big! *Think* big! *Act* big! *Be* big!" By the time we had landed, the man was in a different frame of mind.

There it is. You can even be a coach to a total stranger! One entry point, one teachable moment presents itself, and you step in. It may happen in a conversation with a neighbor's child or a friend's relative or an employee of someone else that you plant the seed. When something draws you to a person, trust that feeling. Share your vision, like Norman did. You may be creating a turning point in that person's life. For the real difference in coaching is not about talent. Or personality. Or pride. Or ambition. It's about your believing in someone. And then doing whatever it takes to help that person be his or her very best. God Bless!

Ken Blanchard and Don Shula

ABOUT THE AUTHORS

Ken Blanchard is an internationally known management consultant, teacher, and co-author of *The One Minute Manager*, which has sold over 9 million copies. He has written and co-authored twenty other books, including his most recent best-seller, *High Five! The Magic of Working Together*, with Sheldon Bowles, Don Carew, and Funicer Paris-Carew. Blanchard and his wife, Margie, founded The Ken Blanchard Companies in 1979 and have consulted for Disney, Honda, Kodak, The Gap, and numerous other entrepreneurial and nonprofit enterprises. They live in San Diego and have two grown children who work with their companies.

Don Shula led the Miami Dolphins to five Super Bowl appearances and the Baltimore Colts to one—more than any other head coach in NFL history. *Sports Illustrated* magazine named Shula its 1993 Sportsman of the Year in honor of his becoming the winningest coach in NFL history. A Hall of Fame Coach, Shula is the only coach to guide a team (the Miami Dolphins) through an undefeated NFL season (17–0 in 1972). He retired from the coaching ranks in January 1996, after 25 years as head coach of the Dolphins. Today, his Shula's Steak Houses are considered among the finest restaurants of their kind in the United States. Coach Shula lives in Miami with his wife, Mary Anne, and is the father of five grown children.

SERVICES AVAILABLE

Ken Blanchard and Don Shula are available to speak to conventions and organizations on the C.O.A.C.H. concepts. In addition, these concepts can be brought alive in your organization and personal life through audiotapes and videotapes. For information on these products and programs, or about Ken Blanchard's availability, contact:

The Ken Blanchard Companies
125 State Place
Escondido, CA 92029
760.489.5005
800.728.6000

For information on Don Shula's availability, contact:

Shula's Hotel & Golf Club
Attention: Bill Herman
6842 Main Street
Miami Lakes, FL 33014
305.820.8035